NEXT-LEVEL INVESTING

NEXT-LEVEL INVESTING

GRETA ROSE

CONTENTS

CHAPTER 1

Introduction

A new era of next-level investing is fast approaching. Instead of simply looking for superior businesses, executives, assets, or earnings, forward-thinking investors are hunting for complicated infrastructures, revolutionary technologies, and massive demographic themes which are all coming to a head over the next decade. The future is about identifying and capitalizing on the next billion-dollar trends. In this essay, we will highlight a few overarching trends influencing all aspects of new economy investing in the next ten years. Each essay in this series will dive into one thematic trend and its transformative consequences over the next decade.

This new era of technological growth and interconnected world markets is making it possible to create massive industrial and consumer infrastructures that we could only dream of just a few decades ago. Many of these big picture themes are only just starting to gather steam and could have major social and economic implications by the time it is said and done. Sometimes finding these trends comes down to a synthesis of browsing through enough economic data and trying as hard as possible to "connect the dots". But one of the key strategies to developing billion-dollar insights is simply asking the right questions, and this is the best place to start.

CHAPTER 2

Understanding the Dynamics of Billion-Dollar Trend

Billion-dollar companies are created around trends – massive, industry-changing shifts that are reshaping the business world. Billions are poured into these future unicorns each year, and the gains made by investing early in one of these companies can be astronomical. But, before we can invest in these next-generation giants, we need to figure out what our next investment should be. This is why I have spent so much time studying trends; they are the single most profitable investment studs that we can follow today. At a very high level, we can define a trend as a lasting change that impacts multiple industries or parts of the world. This enduring shift is caused by multiple factors and has the potential to be as large as billions of dollars.

What makes a trend though? Not every change constitutes one. It must be a change that has multiple industries (or parts of the world) impacted by the same thing. A move up in interest rate by either the FED or Senate has an impact on that particular industry, but not others. The Internet of Things changes transportation, communication, robotics, food, healthcare, legal work, energy, and more. Which is the second point of a good trend: it must be multiple industries. When even one big change is going to impact an entire industry, it could shift the competitive landscape enough to create the next billion-dollar opportunity. These are ideal conditions for our investments. The one area usually overlooked is once an industry-changing shift gains traction and proves to be incredibly valuable, the number of competitors usually follows in an attempt to gain prized market share. This can also cause massive oversupply and be carefully managed. This is the single most profitable type of investment outside of trends, and investing around one or more of these is considered speculative in nature (perhaps more on this in a separate post). As many of these examples support, trends can massively turn into billion-dollar opportunities. However, many "bubble stocks" were trading on incredibly high potential assumptions driven by these same factors. Thus, long-term trends that drive enduring changes are, above all, an investment in value. They are the difference between a fundamental profit driver and nothing more than a fad.

Defining Billion-Dollar Trends

When one trend has already established its roots, there would be coded signs in the grey area about what the next more significant trend could evolve into, maybe in a rough manner. However, defining a vast area that has not been touched upon the concept or the sectors could be a bit of a challenge. There are millions of things happening from the pocket to the planet, and we hardly have any grain of knowledge about the concept as a whole. Despite some attempt, we can only get a bit of an idea. So then, what is a billion-dollar trend? The phrase is self-explanatory: a trend that is expected to grow a business that big.

In other words, it will create a million dollars in revenue quickly and still have significant potential left on the table, making it a sweet spot for investing to capitalize on the growth. However, there is no rule that the billion-dollar trend will always go on to make that much money, and no sector-wide release of information and research on what actually will or will not break the free. It is difficult to identify trends that are expected to be a billion-dollar trend because they will depend on market factors, policies, technologies, costs, and many other factors that are hard to encode in the first place. But it's always possible to guess a little bit of what might happen in the future, right? That's why it's time to look at the broader trends that are moving us, the eyebrow, underlying the major players that are positioned in the sector, the problem-solving approach, and the policies of regional countries.

Factors Driving the Growth of Billion-Dollar Markets
Even when there is a rapid and steep drop-off in the fortunes of some of the early entrants to the space, the cannabis market's scale and potential are difficult to overstate. The global market reached over $50 billion in 2019, and global spending on legal cannabis is expected to grow from $10.2 billion (2018) to $97.35 billion by 2026. In 2017, the digital marketing industry was worth about $241 billion and is projected to balloon to almost $398 billion by 2021. While the hype surrounding cryptocurrencies may have cooled, many aspects of blockchain technology seem to have promise, and companies entering the blockchain space raised billions of dollars through ICOs (initial coin offerings) in short order. By 2030, the market for robotics will likely reach $2.7 trillion, with an 11% growth rate year over year.

The meteoric growth across these widely varied sectors appears to defy simple, unifying explanation. To this end, entrepreneurs, investors, and advisors working in and monitoring these fast-growing spaces cite a confluence of factors that will likely drive billion-dollar markets forward in 2020 and beyond. Increasing public and private investment dollars have gone toward a few, very large players, and this trend is expected to accelerate, driving considerable growth in top-line figures. For some industries, potential growth is mirrored by decreases in underlying technology costs, which allows more companies to begin working with these technologies and ultimately improves their accessibility to small and medium-sized businesses and everyday consumers. Consumer interest is spurring growth in a number of industries, with the market projections for cannabis in particular showing consumers' readiness, with government approval, to spend large amounts of money on a completely new market.

Identifying Sustainable vs. Fad Trends
Investors looking to profit from potential future billion-dollar markets or products must distinguish between fad trends and sustainable trends. They must properly understand the current market context and forecast future socio-economic conditions. Identifying longer-term trends is also crucial for ensuring the relevance of business operations or services. Trends such as healthy products, energy-efficient goods, and digital-oriented technology would persist in the future. The process of trend-spotting does not follow any one ready-made formula. Some of these techniques include crowdsourcing—group opinions provide better insight, and beyond quantitative analysis of economic variables, qualitative and ethical judgment ought to be in order. Factors such as environmental, social, and corporate governance should also be considered.

Long-lasting trends stand in contrast to fads. Trend-spotting techniques may not accurately forecast future markets. Due to these constraints, many investment analysts suggest focusing on sectors that are resilient to the impacts of long-lasting trends; the forecasts derived from the latter can't control consumer spending. A fad or a bubble derives its existence from the misguided beliefs of the crowds. It is practically really random. On the contrary, long-lasting trends have an actual foundation. If one can spot a real trend and its timing, it can indeed give them an advantage. Trend-spotting involves a move from the quantitative analysis and interpretation of patterns to the subtle, culturally embedded nature of fashions. Our society, McLuhan avers, is one of the fashions. In order to manage in an economic climate of shortening innovation cycles, we must recognize patterns of change.

CHAPTER 3

Research and Analysis Techniques for Identifying F

Ronology (The Jolly Swagmen) Group's version 1.0 of the Next Level Investment Toolkit with the "Investing in Billion Dollar Opportunities" framework is located here. The skills required to build machine learning models using the Python ecosystem are minuscule compared to the a-priori processing that's needed to identify lucrative and desirable investments. Our platforms break this process down into steps, teach you how to automate them, quantify them, and deploy and iterate these strategies at scale.

Most top-quartile venture capital investors owe equally very little to their financial modeling skills and instead depend upon the metaphysical prowess of their proprietary deal flow. In simple terms, there are multiple ways to skin a cat. However, when it comes to evaluating the size of the total addressable market in the current world economy vs. past economies, LKS states, "there's reason to believe that almost all new markets are interesting - and potentially very large, like in >$1 billion dollar large. This is in part because of network effects, but mainly because the most valuable companies in today's economy are technology-based."

But how, by use of which exact analysis techniques, documentation and data collection methods to we pinpoint these? There are many examples in the investment hemisphere. Many investors when citing good investments explain the benefit of "skate to where the puck is going, not where it has been." In order to do so with some measure of accuracy you need to find those future billion-dollar trends first. Decadal trends are pervasive and you need to become a first-minute-marty, or the next first minute lotto aficionado.

Market Research Strategies

Today, Shark Tank fans and venture capitalist investors alike would give anything to be able to go back in time and invest in companies like Apple or Tesla. To predict where the next billion-dollar opportunity lies, angel investors and venture capitalists often leverage strategies and market research tactics specific to identifying what future opportunities might be the next hot commodity. According to "The Granularity of Growth: How to Identify the Sources of Growth and Drive Enduring Company Performance" by Strategy& and PwC, the 3 market research strategies below are commonly used by investors in high-growth sectors to uncover future billion-dollar opportunities.

This strategy involves identifying major shifts in the world that are mere blips on the radar. Companies and market conditions can be quickly and dramatically shaped and impacted by forces outside their control. According to the PwC report, 72% of 2,605 business and technology executives globally believe they have good governance and ethics approaches. To accomplish this, your investment thesis must be date-time stamped, and only valid both two or five years down the road and in the present. For example, facial recognition is absolutely exploding into everything imaginable right now.

This should be part of your narrative's theme. "Facial recognition is absolutely exploding into everything imaginable right now."

Data Analysis Tools and Techniques

Most analysts and investors dive into a wide variety of prospective new trends by using numerical data to create a direct comparison – whether it is on the occurrence of a key phrase mentioned over the past few years, the net inflow of institutional money to an industry, or the sector capitalization against others. Invented, as a result of these mind-boggling variety of associated tools and processes in the field, are some niche tools too, in order to facilitate an analysis of potential opportunities. As such, advanced tools such as the stock screener, Excel and AI software, Excel add-ins, Excel links and correlation analysis (in particular, a correlation heat map) are used through the Beating the Street ethos, in order to extract important data for effective decision making.

The stock screener or 'stock filter' is a tool that enables an investor to look for shares based on a specific criteria or metric like a minimum ROA, ROE or EPS/PE ratio. Ultimately, investors can scan the market for companies that possess the capacity to develop to multi-bag potential. On the other hand, Excel and AI software is often used to store data in a user-friendly environment. Also, wizard-based systems can help you pinpoint the stock to buy using the power of Excel and Bigdata. Using single, simple if statements, data is often virtually compared. If you have a degree of aptitude in spreadsheets, strong knowledge of an industry & a feel for data mining – Excel can be your weapon! Moreover, Excel add-ins allow small tools such as accessing interest rates files and statistics. The data analysis tool in Excel can be used to isolate key data points in a table, such as a filtering process. Data analysis links allow data to be linked i.e. to feed into the software easily and correlation tools can easily compare their relationship with a quick glance.

Industry Expert Interviews

Industry expert interviews were used to excel our capability in uncovering future billion-dollar opportunities in the cannabis, alternative works, and psychedelics space. Over the course of multiple weeks, we organized interviews with official and under-the-radar business heads, key opinion makers, researchers, and visionaries who have profound industry experience and specialization in their respective fields. Our proprietary survey aimed to extract the best databases from our labels. Surprisingly, only a reduced section of the total answers were transformed into NFTs, despite the interviews being clustered into secluded groups to refine the data.

At this juncture, our most robust tactic is to understand outlying future-value trends across several verticals, including psychedelics, cannabis, and purposeful workspaces between genomics healthcare, longevity, connectivity, and the 'human experience.' Our expert interviews help us acknowledge the position of the digital revolution impacting healthcare and the psychedelics space at present. Previously, our records identified the risks. These records lay down a multibillion-dollar prospective worth at different parts of their value chains, frequently by investigating potential integration points where applicable. This is an attempt to popularize the richest knowledge we could source for these options.

CHAPTER 4

Case Studies of Successful Investments in Emerging

The natural language generation is such a powerful technology that it is already eliminating the need to have expert insights on a continuous basis. Just take a look at the case studies that I have presented above to demonstrate how AI technologies have enabled embracing billion-dollar trends without expert advice.

Do you have to use expert advice to invest in the next global trend set to be worth one billion dollars or more in the future? As you can see from the above case studies, the answer is clearly no. For instance, you could just pay attention to market data. However, an investment manager would be able to discover the next set of opportunities far faster than the startups that brought these markets to light if they leveraged artificial intelligence and spindle technology to process gargantuan amounts of market insight. And the earlier you were to invest in that trend, the higher your returns would be.

Tech Sector Innovations

Firms that have invented recent tech sector innovations are not only leading their niche markets but are also growing immensely at triple-digit compounds. What has made Tesla "The chosen one"?

Robotic cars certainly, but Tesla has Sirius, Tesla Energy for Solar Wall (in 100+ countries), Tesla TV, and Netflixlytics. Companies like Facebook or Twitter also seem like a simple idea. Who thought they would become multi-hundred-billion-dollar companies? How did they grow to that scale? These may become your-million-dollar-questions for our three next-level ventures.

The "tech" sector is commonly considered young, beginning its exponential growth since Apple developed the iPod in 2001; the online and software world has grown at a correlated rate since. However, most people do not know we have seen recent tech capability and "true innovation" since we stood on the ground; 3D printing has been popular in China since 2011-12. The most crowded, crazy competition is seen in the latest e-toy, electric car, and Amazon-delivery-drone vertical-integrated areas. Very often over-capacity and constant new-product development mean a lack of profitability. Capex to cope with capacity makes it hard to recover costs from some older product ranges. Associating the new and old groups under one listed company makes valuations problematic. Biotechs also fail to be listed, suffer high R&D and wrong-way risk, and do not cover costs. Facing death is not liberating the creatives.

Healthcare and Biotech Breakthroughs

After some years, you should sell your learning stock for a much bigger share of the profits. Even $1,000 would yield a 12,300% return on investment, turning your initial $8 investment into $66 billion. That's the untapped potential involved in finding learning stocks that cater to future billion-dollar industries.

2019 provided real-world examples of how big of an impact healthcare and biotech breakthroughs can have in terms of profits and market potential. This "is the century of biology," said Derek Jantz of Zacks Investment Research. He estimated that cell and gene therapy sales would total $2 billion in 2019 and were expected to surge to $14 billion in 2024. At least half a dozen companies that went public in 2018 and 2019 combined were working on gene editing or gene therapy treatments targeting liver diseases, according to a Boston Globe report.

IPO investors who bought Genmab at its debut in 2000 would have had a 3,100% return on investment by 2019. At an IPO price of $29.94, a $10,000 investment in May 2016 with dividends reinvested would have turned into $29,299 a year later after Bristol-Myers Squibb acquired cancer drugmaker Medarex. "I made more this year on one deal than I've made in the last 10 years," Peter Kolchinsky said at the time. At the close of 2019, Regeneron stock had increased 30% so far that year, from $335 to $434, due to its binding agreement with the Trump administration to develop a vaccine for the coronavirus. After a 60% two-day stock surge on November 9 and 10, 2020, Pfizer's market capitalization increased by $25 billion.

Sustainable Energy Solutions

Let's see how a few investors capitalized on their hunch that sustainable energy solutions were going to be the next big thing.

Starting today, the solar panel industry is expected to grow by 107.4% in revenue in the United States alone, reaching some 23.6 billion dollars by 2027. Yet despite the recent success, the industry currently produces just 3.3% of America's 20 trillion kWh annual energy consumption. Despite the plant having been such an investment success, the real success, for both HSL and other solar park investors, has been its impact on the world. The Minworth plant is currently believed to be reducing CO_2 emissions by 2,500 tonnes a year. Over the next 30 years, this adds up to over 100,000 tonnes. It produces sufficient electricity to serve 750 UK homes in a year (203m kWh). For other investors, the desire to save energy bought or generated by solar is propelling battery technologies like Tesla's Powerwall towards the billion-dollar mark. Home power storage generated just 300 million dollars in the US this year, but industry experts estimate it will hit a billion by next year and fifteen billion by 2024. In credit, the burgeoning interest has encouraged investment with the carbon bond market growing by 82% between 2006 and 2020 to reach 214 billion dollars.

As the writing is on the roof, there have been new billion-dollar investments in the sustainable energy sector. Bioenergy has also gone solar in the UK with Drax (formerly North-East England's industrial energy provider) converting its last coal-fired unit into biomass capacity. The giant unit located in Selby "forms part of the largest decarbonization project in Europe" and is said to be generating carbon savings greater than 80 percent. Another two biomass units in North Yorkshire called the Drax Power Station are expected to be generating enough electricity to serve four million homes after the latest conversion project is completed. Developing the alternative energy sector has also pushed the company into billion-dollar status with today's conversion projects accounting for approximately 700 million pounds of planned capital investment.

CHAPTER 5

Risk Management Strategies for Investing in High-G

Entering and investing in high growth sectors always carries risks. The time horizons and volatility of ideation, implementation, and consumer adoption are hard to project for most innovative sectors. A few risk management strategies that can be used to mitigate risks when investing as the sector goes through this phase could be: staying highly diversified, using protective put options, or keeping reduced positions in the sector until it is more established.

Dividing investments across different industries and spaces can be a good risk management strategy, as one can diversify both at the industry and the company level. This can be a great way to own companies in new, high growth sectors without taking all of the sector-specific risk, allowing for more room for investment. Options are considered to be a derivative, and while they are often used for speculation, there are many great options strategies used for risk management. One strategy that can be used for previously established trades and to manage risk and continue holding positions can be using protective put options. This would involve placing a protective put a few percentage points beyond any established support level in the stock. Then, if the shares get stopped out, the put would go up in price so that the chance of losing shares of stock would be lower. Then when/if the shares of the stock increased in price, the investor would be able to sell the protective put options to lock in gains. If the protective put option expires while the stock price is higher than the strike price, then the cost of the option can be lower than the potential profit. This could be a great way to protect a stock investment in a previously worse established sector while waiting for another sector to pick up.

Diversification and Portfolio Allocation

Because investment can be unpredictable, it is important for any risk management strategy to rely as little on luck as possible. Diversification is a simplified and familiar concept, where investors attempt to spread their risk across multiple, unrelated securities, so that the success of one does not solely determine the success of the investor. By integrating a variety of securities, the resultant volatility should stabilize and stock risk will demonstrate a closer adherence to its mean. Put into practical terms, the investment portfolio should contain an equal number of consumer discretionary, consumer staples, energy, financial, health care, industrial, materials, technology, and utility stocks according to the S&P 500 Global Industry Classification Standard. But simply being diversified does not suffice, as the financial crisis of 2008 demonstrates. That is where portfolio allocation across sectors becomes crucial.

Investors wishing to speculate on potential growth need access to different sectors to cushion risk. But, as the NASDAQ bubble revealed, reliance on one sector is one of the riskiest approaches to investing. The solution lies in allocating an equally concentrated investment portfolio across multiple sectors, not individual companies. Assuming that long-term growth and success are not mutually exclusive with fundamental analysis, this paper evaluates the risk and returns of both methods to determine the practical benefits and disadvantages of stock trading and investment in the S&P 500.

Hedging Strategies

Outlook: While experts might disagree on what the top short-term startup trends will be, few dispute cognitive technology, bio-computing, biometrics, diagnostics, and mobile medical devices' potential over the next decade. Outside of short-term trading tactics like options strangles/straddles, put spreads and buying deep ITM covered calls, holding options as a hedging strategy (as well as using cash secured puts to buy into options) might be a good strategy as startups and other tech companies in general are not immune to the growth pains associated with high growth sectors. This pain can come in the form of large pullbacks from lofty highs as well as rampant news hype that might (or might not) affect the company in question.

Prospective Options: Investors interested in protecting their investment can buy put options, use a put spread or create a call option as a "synthetic put." While not an ideal strategy for purely hedging, one could also short the stock. Shorting could also be used as a hedged position if the loss from the stock was limited by holding a protective put and the call premium received covered the loss in the stock. If stock was to rally and an investor was put the stock to cover short calls, then being short stock could be hedged with a call option or buy back stock and sell the call. If discussing futures as a hedge, other ways to protect a stock include futures & options on indices (options such as the SPY) or other relevant sectors. These instruments can be a trade-off between diversifying away company-specific risk while giving up portfolio-specific risk and the increase in correlation between all asset classes. Options & futures can also have their own unique risks to consider when hedging.

Stress Testing and Scenario Analysis

Stress tests combined with scenario analysis can unlock valuable insights into any investment under various conditions. They allow investors and management to stress-test various assumptions as part of a holistic approach to managing risks in today's high-growth sectors. In this appendix, we cover stress tests and scenario analysis to give readers a conceptual overview of the tools we use to identify and mitigate potential risks in new opportunities outside traditional cash-flow prediction and control. We aim to bring our readers up to date on what we view as a new paradigm for investment risk. In our experience, investment managers have been best served by adopting a holistic approach.

Stress Test A stress test is a simulation of how a given variable or event will affect performance under an adverse set of parameters. It is commonly used in economics and engineering to predict the collapse of a given system due to a variety of possible inputs. It is widely used in the banking and insurance sectors to ensure exposure to rare but high-impact events is not excessive. Strictly speaking, stress tests examine any aspect of a business that is not going according to plan or modeling negatively. A list of potential factors of business risk is shown below. Note that it is by no means an exhaustive list, and in our conversations with investors, we've heard many other great risks at play. We aim to simulate some of these issues based on our read of current market information.

CHAPTER 6

Regulatory and Compliance Considerations in Next-L

Preparing to engage as a next-level investor takes more than just understanding good ethics or well-articulated business practices. Since the primary mechanism of profit in next-level investing is valuation capture - the process of ensuring that the companies we're investing in can be seen through so as to ensure that their investments in themselves can drive high premium - the exercise of simultaneity is crucial. Simultaneity is the process of which we ensure that all stakeholders are aware of the truth so that the company is self-aware enough to be the most attractive one in the market. For future valuation purposes, cost as an externality has to go to zero. Decreasing cost reduces risks for the company - a fundamental principle in investing.

It is possible to indicate that a company does participate in such stakeholder capitalism by either ensuring and demonstrating that their costs are indeed zero or showing through proxy data why they are unable to conceive of a world where that is possible or relevant. Through the UN Global Compact, companies can share with the public formal and open documentation of their internal cost of compliance to regulations that confirm the company does not invest enough in itself to require a positive valuation on the basis that it is simply too risky. This is similar to saying that companies can now articulate their SEC all-in corroborated regulatory cost. When assessing where to invest, we can show a process of establishing collaborative stakeholder partnerships to explore how leading companies in particular sectors transformed strategic risk management and leading ESG performance outcomes beyond regulatory compliance toward resiliency and strategic advantage.

CHAPTER 7

Ethical and Social Responsibility in High-Growth I

Global investing patterns show a focus and emphasis on more ethical and responsible investment options. One of the chief segments enjoying unprecedented growth is blockchain and cryptocurrency. This is the future of not just investment, but other ideas such as healthcare, governing, retail design, and beyond. Environmental technology and biotech is also booming and is expected to break the billion-dollar investments in the near future as it plays a crucial role in the future promises of reducing pollution and eradication of diseases through gene editing. Without a doubt, investing in these areas would have cash inflow in the future, but our high-growth investments must also focus on social responsibility. No one wants to invest in casinos, deadly cyber weapons, or high-stakes bacon slot machines if it comes to the cost of our future.

Being responsible while investing in high-growth areas is now becoming a future trend. Everyone can contribute to the beginning of a new decade in societal tensions. While putting money into education and clean energy savings to make a happy world may sound good, going against toxic industries regarding cultural priorities is not only ethically upright yet is the key to investing in future billions. The shape of our future is largely dictated by finance. Let's continue to place our money where we think our future is.

CHAPTER 8

The Role of Technology in Identifying and Capitali

Technology has indeed assisted investors in identifying trends such as the luxury market, electric vehicles, and cryptocurrencies as potential multi-year, even billion-dollar trends. These AI-powered investment strategies could result in a sign-up process that closely rivals the enjoyment of 'window shopping,' as users foresee their own features and preferences coming to life in investing style. These possibilities and advances have been referred to as a way of identifying and potentially capitalizing on future trends. Additionally, they have been suggested for users interested in investment opportunities or trends.

There are countless attitudes and beliefs one can develop, too many to address in a simple article, as trends this decade could create several additional trillion-dollar opportunities. However, future trillion-dollar sectors include advancements in aging, longevity, and regenerative medicine, as well as environmental trends such as carbon capture, global reforestation of specific tree species, and lab-grown meats. Investors likely understand broad trends but might not be abreast of the many burgeoning ideas in their early stages. Additionally, many trends are derived from shifting cultural attitudes, too unpredictable for any money management program to truly determine. As trends in finance typically require multiple years to grow from seedling ideas into billion-dollar industries, present-day methodologies do not adequately provide confidence levels in identification and expected returns.

CHAPTER 9

Global Perspectives on Billion-Dollar Opportunitie

Consumer healthcare products in Africa and beyond Health-care and beauty are two very substantial markets in Africa, and international companies have long explored opportunities in these sectors. The value of an investment opportunity rests largely on the dearth of competition and increasing market growth, both sentiments shared by Asoko and Africa Exchange. They operate in Nigeria and have confidence in the burgeoning manufacturing and distribution of baby, family, and medicinal products. Africa Exchange aims to raise $2 million from the initial 4 investors at $500,000 per share for 30%.

Geração TUDO Menino Mozambique In Mozambique, there is little diverse and frequent out-of-school teaching and entertainment services available to children, young people, and even adults. Some programs are specialized. Such a centered model is not particularly linked to the catering, fashion, and cosmetic product-selling franchises. With these franchises and assistance known as Generation TUDO, we are catering for a variety of additional students. The Geração TUDO is providing consumers between the ages of 8 and 12 with enjoyable activities. Operate a beauty salon, a fashion house, and a renowned pizzeria. The BOTDE operates an international support model, with plans to grow into a larger region, beginning with the southern West Australia region. Telstra also has the right to expand into a cooperation with the franchisor in the field of the Botder. The market approach is focused on the primary school, preschool, and leisure fields.

CHAPTER 10

The Future of Investing: Trends and Predictions

Over the last 5 years, investing has seen exponential growth. New products, platforms, and resources are now available to enable everyone to fully participate in the stock market, evolving past the legacy of investing being a luxury reserved only for the financial elite. Cryptocurrency (and the NFT wave) are revolutionizing both currency and investment as we embark upon the digital age. With changing landscapes but the same end goals, join us in predicting the future of investing and, ultimately, what you should and shouldn't invest in.

The Future of the Meme Economy and Meme Stocks Similarly, companies like MemeTeam and YOLO Stocks have raised millions in their seed rounds and funneled that money into the stock market on behalf of their users. That's to say that the meme economy is only going to get bigger and meme stocks are guaranteed to be a part of it. While investing in the stock market can yield high returns, the climate and tangible trade of NFTs can have even higher returns. Last year, Christine Aje, who is a program manager at British high street bank NatWest, stumbled across a tweet that decade-old news website NowThis shared. In keeping with her principles, Christine used

"Kedarkissme" as a PFP and posted the link to OpenSea on the internet. Three days later, the link was sold to a fourth Musk brother: Elon. If you play games like Roblox or VRChat, some of the pixel art and avatars that are gaining revered infamy in the NFT ether may have some real value—for now.

CHAPTER 11

Conclusion and Key Takeaways

Looking at the conversation from different angles, do not let sticking with replacement asset prices and hesitating about possessed cryptassets on the balance to side-track from delving into the fundamentals. To your own minds, do not fall into the trap of guessing today's novelty's demand and following it mechanically. Thinking is your "edge". We all know that next-level investing will turn careful thinkers into billionaires, pondering what is possible and likely to turn into a billion-dollar trend in the years ahead - predicting, front-running, and reaping the rewards of sticking with the leading choice of civilization.

To truly understand and benefit from all that was elaborated on in both parts, one needs to start every academic question like these from philosophy. First principles thinking, every single time. Big upheavals and transformations challenge the way we used to think about fundamental stuff yesterday, e.g. new goods and services we might be spending our money on in 5-10 years, the tenth decade of this third millennium. The best practice and cutting-edge way to transfer societal wealth over time, the Prosperity System that adjusts and will make due in order for similarly welfaring stakeholders to have lives. Actions and economies based heavily on Digital are and will be continually morphing our prominent sociotechno-economic shift.